Verses from the
Unseen

Claire Louise Streatfield

BookLeaf
Publishing

India | USA | UK

Presentation by *BookLeaf Publishing*

Web: www.bookleafpub.com

E-mail: info@bookleafpub.com

ISBN: 9789358314182

First edition 2024

DEDICATION

For my dad. We wrote poems together once.

ACKNOWLEDGEMENT

A massive thank you to all who've lent a hand, shared wisdom, or sparked inspiration along my path so far. Your support, whether big or small, has left an indelible mark on me and my creative endeavours.

To any unsuspecting readers who stumbled upon this book - your curiosity is profoundly appreciated. I hope these pages bring a smile to your face, or at least an expression of intrigued agreement, as you read along.

Plus a final subtle nod to my high school, whose unwavering dedication to academic subjects like science inadvertently fuelled that spark of creative rebellion within me.

PREFACE

Within these 21 poems lies a medley of randomness that might leave you a tad bewildered, perhaps even teetering on the brink of boredom. Fear not, for their brevity offers a swift journey through this curious mishmash. Embrace the peculiar, the haphazard, and in their fleeting moments, discover a glimpse of amusement or a spark of introspection amidst the ordinary.

Better

It's so quiet
I wonder why, yet can't remember a time when
it wasn't
Is this normal now?
Has my brain given up?
No more commentary or thinking or butting in
when I don't want it to
But also no more ideas, no imagination, no
amusing inappropriate thoughts
Just silence
That's OK, this could be fun
Meditation 24/7
Mindfulness, emptiness, nothingness
But it's so very quiet…..
Perhaps I'm in mourning
Silence as a mark of respect?
Perhaps I should fill it again, with emotions and
feelings and random stuff
So it's bursting at the seams,
Ah, a memory…bursting, full, loud
So very loud
That was the problem wasn't it?
That's why we thought it best to be quiet
But it's lonely in the silence
And dark, cold and kind of robotic

I could just let a little bit in this time
Maybe a melody
Yes, a melody, that's it
Never alone with music playing
That's much better
I shall stay here, alone with the sound, until I am
ready
It soothes the void and turns up the dimmer
switch
A little brighter
A little more
That's better

Not every loss brings a sorrow

I didn't wake up one day to find you suddenly
gone
It was a gradual parting of ways
Gently and quietly you slipped from my life
Over months, not hours or days

I didn't even notice you fading at first
Although there was slight indication
Despite subtle hints and signs
I thought I must be mistaken

I was slowly exhaling you out of my lungs
Breath by breath, this development happened
Vanishing fragments leaving me feeling changed
Not sure if I should even feel saddened

But not every loss brings a sorrow
And this one is not to be mourned
Memories and photos to keep you alive
And no need to be upset or forlorn

Looking back I can see that you just had to go
No good for me or my mind

But it's strange getting used to the absence of
you
And the fact that I'm left here, behind

Didn't want to believe, but now I can see it
The proof is in front of my eyes
Standing here without you it's obvious
I definitely need a smaller size

A tale of 2 different tails

Let's go, let's explore, quick!!
Race round and round, stick our head in that
hole
We might find treasure
Or food. The best treasure.

Let's stay put, let's freeze, stand still!
Or check. Check the perimeter, quick!
What was that? What's that noise?
It's not the time for food.

It's getting away, let's chase, come on!
Follow until we can't see home,
Such adventure! We're losing it, it's gone
What could we have found? Maybe food.

It's not safe, stay put, stay alert
Quiet, I heard something, ssshhh
Who's that? What if they hurt us?
Stay still, stay invisible.

Round the corner, what could it be?
Maybe food? Or friends or a big surprise!
Rush towards it, head first, into the breach…
Best day ever. Maybe food

Hold back, in the shadows, by the wall
Peak round, is it safe?
I'm not sure…we should stay here
Where it's quiet. No adventures

But maybe food…..

Is it really?

"No parking. Entrance in constant use"

Traffic in and out, in and out

Twenty-four hours a day

Long queues stretch down the street

Eager to get in

Then out again

Endless stream

Constant.

Nope

Never your intention

Another night arrives.
This time, I will stay inside
Retreat into the darkness.
In distant moments past
I craved for us to be torn apart
Yet all of it remains.

I'm glad I can't, often I'm glad I won't
Never your intention
You desire nothing, I did nothing at all
Never your intention

I'm silent with those who'll listen
The anticipation still lingers;
Everything is alive with sensation.
In my undamaged vessel
All that endures is intensified
And I'm beginning to float.

I'm glad I can't, often I'm glad I won't
Never your intention
You desire nothing, I did nothing at all
Never your intention
I'm glad I can't, often I'm glad I won't
Never your intention

You desire nothing, I did nothing at all
Never your intention
Never your intention
Never your intention
Never your intention
Never

My song

In a tiny moment, mundanity was broken
Not just broken, blasted through

Head lifted, ears widened as if to funnel the
sound as quickly as I could
Couldn't hear it fast enough, yet didn't want it to
ever end

Brain glowing, breathing held.
Cheeks lifted, eyes crinkled, smile wide
This is it

Building, sweeping
Reverbing, blending
Enveloped in the distortion
Belonging to the sound
I live here now

The game

There's a fun game I like to play sometimes
When I'm bored right out of my brain
To find some really cool band names
From stuff that's super mundane

The rules are they have to be written
So on signs, or labels or prose
But once you start seeing them it's so hard to
stop
They're everywhere, right under your nose

The best ones make it onto a list
To save up for the day I find fame
I'll have started a band and we're so very cool
And we need a crazy mysterious name

I'd give you examples but most are too good to
share
Can't give them away...sorry
In case one day I'm trawling on Spotify
And find you've stolen Shoebill Canoe Safari

Encouragement for the weak

In a room full of people silently counting to 10
Inside their heads as bodies force pulleys and
bars,
Encased in energetic green walls and wipe-clean
surfaces
Contained by reflections of every angle.
A soundtrack of mid-volume generic beats
plays,
Heard but never listened to

From behind arms in sculpted fold, Arnie's eyes
meet mine
"You earn your body" he shouts as I read
Encouragement for the weak

Where once unassuming words take on new
powerful meanings;
Goblet, curtsy, shrug.
A new language, of lifting corpses and Eastern
European destinations.
Cast-iron discs of happiness are shunted and
rolled
Deployed like giant metal happy pills
Success measured by pushing and pulling
Celebrated in 5's and 10s

"Just one more rep"
Encouragement for the weak

Instagram aspirations draw people in
With false promises of glossy fitness dreams
Moulded by iron and time into tangible triumph
Unveiling substance beneath the shine
Raw and addictive

"It never gets easier; you just get stronger"
Encouragement for the weak

There is a tree

There is a tree
It's kind of a big deal
But it's not famous
you can't google it and find pages of glossy
images
It doesn't have a Wikipedia page
And isn't on the socials, not even a hashtag
Influencers and hippies don't pose for selfies
with it
But it is my most favourite tree in the whole
world
A symbol of clinging on

Thousands of people pass it by everyday
I wonder if any even notice
It grows without pot or soil
Not even near the ground
A headstart on height
It has no right to be there
But grows regardless
Unapologetic
Fearless

As the train rolls in
I look up to catch a glimpse

Thriving against the odds
Some hope for us all
This is my reminder
Open your eyes and you might find your own
So, to my tree:
I see you
And I thank you

Spotify Sadness

Sad songs, Sad Bops, Life Sucks
Sad girl starter pack

Sad hour, Broken, Coping with loss
Heartbreaker, Heartache

Alone again, Tear drop, Classics for crying
Cry Sleep Repeat

Sad country drinking, Less sad country drinking
Day drinking: Sad
End in tears

I'm still upset but i forgive you
I'm not crying, you are
F**k love

Winter

This time it will be different

I won't be surprised by the darkness
Creeping in like a pantomime villain
It has an appointment, and it's in the diary
Scrawled in slight annoyance like a trip to the
dentist
Not how you'd add a fancy foreign holiday
With a playful font, and cutesy little hearts
Just "Winter begins"

But, this time it will be different

I will counter with light of my own
Prescribed and dispensed each day
Sad lamps for morning to take off the edge
Come evening, ignite what I can, stare into
flames
Add a twinkling of fairy lights for the magic
Mull anything that moves
And blanket myself in fleece

Upgrade my language to warm fuzzy words
Everything snug, toasty, heated and comfy
Become one with the cosy

The mug never set down, just refilled
Kettle on repeat
Mustn't give in to the tired, it's psychological at
best
Disagree with the sun about evening
Six months to convince it's not missed

This time winter and I are friends

Missed connections

It's just sauntered past
Crept along to overtake
An utterly brazen manoeuvre
Our sad useless faces look on
While we're sat motionless and exposed
Yards from the platform
Defeated and helpless
Easy pickings

The room

My belongings must be alive
They're breeding right now, I'm sure
I just turned round from my desk
And can no longer see the door
I'm sure I walked through it once
And under my feet there was floor

Turning back to my desk, that's covered now too
I should never have averted my eyes
Piles and unpiles of this and of that
Growing exponentially in size
While I recognise most as things that I own
I'm still paralysed by surprise

The extent of the clutter is becoming clear
But to it I'm convinced there is more
They're either forming little families,
Or armies and prepping for war,
Fortifying the defences
And exploding from the drawer

I thought I was just being sensible
But was believing my own little lies
That I needed one in every colour
And backups just to be wise

Turns out I was wrong
You can have too many random supplies

No escape now, I'm undeniably trapped
Should've tackled this before
Nipped it all in the bud before it got out of hand
But it was easier to ignore
So I become one with it now, I've accepted this
fate
Might as well stay and explore

Grievances: a list

Impossible to open bacon packets
Rustling plastic bags
Playing music out loud in public
The dinging of bicycle bells

The smell of unflavoured popcorn
Stupid loud modified cars
Gate in constant use sign
Having to queue for the loo

Children laughing or crying
Children's babbling noises
Children

People noisily eating bananas
People noisily eating anything
People

Unmoved

23

Decisions unmade
Frozen thoughts, like ice, can't flow,
Stalled in endless choice

Wilko: a love story

You're gone and I'm left desolate
What utter sadness I can't comprehend
Didn't know it would hit me so hard
It's a loss I just cannot mend
After decades we spent together I'm
Left longing for you to spend
All my money on this and on that
Knew on you I could always depend
For everything needed or not, amazing
Items around every bend
Sorry I could not save you
Never knew I would have to defend
The kingdom of treasures and wonder
Somewhere I would always recommend
It's hard but I must live without you
Only memories remain til the end
I'll miss you but know this, you will
Never be forgotten my friend

60 seconds inside

Memories are weird
Now I'm thinking of a sad singing cat in an
alleyway
There are always so many in crime films,
And underpasses - dodgy meetings next to
graffiti walls
Good Enough by Dodgy came out in 1996

Brains are basically delicate electrical jelly
I prefer pink blancmange in the shape of a rabbit
I've never seen Watership Down
They used balloons in the war to stop aircraft
attacks
Which is wild cos balloons can pop
Diet coke is my favourite but I used to like
Cream Soda

It's true

I travelled round Africa during lockdown
A different country each day
Flitting from Uganda to Ethiopia on a whim
It was so quick and easy
No fellow travellers or airports
I didn't even need a passport
I remember thinking that it was the only way to
travel
Mainly because it was literally the only way to
travel
It was a wild time
Via the medium of coffee beans was a legitimate
airline
Excitement about each new destination was real
So I learned how to make it properly
To honour the well travelled beans
Bought a moka pot
And a frother
Watched videos online
Read about grind and roast
Chose a special cup
Hand-potted in Tintagel
And it felt like a big adventure
Because it was
I travelled round Africa during lockdown

In this place

Stand somewhere where bad things happened
Really feel it, the discomfort
The stale air imprinted with pain
Allow it to fill your lungs until you don't want to
breathe,
The space consumed by it

Stand somewhere where bad things happened
The ground rotten beneath your feet
As if it might collapse into it's own decay
Paralysed by it as it spreads over you, into your
bones
Invisible but palpable

Stand somewhere where bad things happened
There is no romance here
No whispers or shadows of the past,
Just silent pain screaming into the present
Urging you to listen

The incident

I have for you the most modern challenge
To identify brain over technology code
I wrote a poem, AI wrote another
Couldn't choose which one to upload
So I put them both in and meshed them together
I'll call it a collaboration
What started as fun to make something silly
Ended up in me feeling deflation
A ridiculous prompt and an ordinary story
To be woven into words and letter
I'm only annoyed because it was so very clear
The truth is, the fake one is better.

Prompt: write a romantic poem about cleaning
the floor after your dog, Amber, stepped in her
own poo and walked it through the house

Poem 1:

With playful glee she trotted inside
Unaware of what accompanied her dance
Weaving through the house to her favourite spot,
Over surfaces that didn't stand a chance

Paw prints left as souvenirs of her joy,

I smiled before I quite understood
That they were not just muddy impressions
And maybe she'd been up to no-good

One look in her eyes, I knew she'd just made an
error
Didn't mean to bring this indoors
We've all made mistakes, and I'll pay the price
Which in this case is cleaning the floors

As I reach for the cloth and some sweet-smelling
spray
Amber looks on with a quizzical glance
The paw was wiped clean and no harm was
done,
A shared moment of humour perchance?

Poem 2:

In mishap's wake, amidst the fray,
Our dear Amber in playful display,
With steps untamed, a journey starts,
Leaving trails of artistry in our hearts.

Through corridors where chaos reigned,
Her playful spirit, love unfeigned,
Yet in her dance, a mess she made,
A canvas laid, love's escapade.

With mop in hand, we take the chore,
In this unexpected dance, we explore,
For as we cleanse each tainted tile,
Love's tender laugh, it does beguile.

The scent of soap, a fragrant spree,
Erases marks, leaves history free,
In each wiped floor, our bond unveiled,
Through canine whims, our love prevailed.

So here we stand, in the aftermath,
In this dance of love, a humorous laugh,
For in this tale of mishaps spun,
Our love endures, two hearts as one.

Did you easily spot, while reading through,
Which was the real, which written by who?
Should we be scared, unplug our devices,
Protect the creative, whatever the prices?

I gave it some thought, considered what this all
meant,
And I'm sure you will all agree
It doesn't mean that computers will take over the
world,
Just that they write poems better than me

I wrote some poems

Sit down and write a poem.
OK. I mean, how hard can that really be?
It's just words put together in a beautiful flow
And remember to rhyme every other line...oh,
dammit.

Failed already. Now, are there rules about line
length?
I can't remember from school
And does that need a comma, or full stop?
I do need a rhyme in here somewhere.....fool

It needs more romance, it's not poemy enough.
As my fingers danced upon silver keys, letters
whirled creating tapestries
Of absolute nonsense. That sounds really naff
Back to the basics...

What is it about?
Something I really enjoy...
Not writing poems

That was a little haiku so it's definitely a poem
now
Or contains one at least, so it fits

And maybe this doesn't count
But I'm taking it and calling it quits